COME & ADORE

AN ADVENT DEVOTIONAL

BY: KRISTI MENASHE

To my Lord and Savior, Jesus Christ, all glory and honor and praise to You alone. To know You and make You known...that is my desire.

Introduction

The Lord works outside of time, and I know that. However, I am a procrastinator. As a college student, I would often wait until the night before a paper was due to begin writing it. When I was in charge of the bills, early on in our marriage, I would often pay them on the due date. (Thank God for auto-pay and that my husband eventually took over!) When our family is headed off on a week-long vacation, our suitcases get pulled down from the rafters the night before we leave. When we travel, our hotels are usually booked around 9pm of the night we would like to stay. I understand that these things would be considered stressful to most. Even when I am telling others about my ways, they cringe, shake their heads, and tell me how they "could never do that!"

I have always enjoyed advent(s). As a kid, I remember lighting the candles on the wreath at the kitchen table each week during the Christmas season. As a parent, I have purchased many an advent calendar over the years. There was even the year I typed out verses, bought little candies and gifts, and made my own. Last year, my mom made an adorable advent for my children. For as long as I can remember, advent has been an important part of our Decembers.

A few years back, the Lord put it on my heart to write an advent devotional. I made some notes and brainstormed a bit, but nothing made it onto paper, print, or social media. (I'm a procrastinator, remember?)

As November of 2019 came to a close, I vividly remember the Lord putting it on my heart to "put myself out there" and to somehow use my Instagram account. On November 30th, His direction was clear. It's often hard to explain to others how

He speaks without sounding crazy, but let me say this: I knew, without a doubt, that the very next day (12/1/19) I was to wake up and wait for Him to give me a word. I would need to get up early. I would need to trust that He would show up (with not only the word itself, but the words to share). Each night, I would battle fleshly anxieties and thoughts: What if He doesn't give me tomorrow's word? What if the words don't flow? What if I sound stupid? What if people unfollow me because they get sick of my Jesus-talk?...and the list goes on.

On December 1st, I knew right away how I would begin. I remember feeling excited, but nervous. Over the following days, I would wake up and by the time my coffee had brewed, He would give me the word. Sometimes, I would hear it before my feet hit the floor. Every morning, I would take a photo (to use as my background) and create a post, using the word that He would lay upon my heart. I would search the Scriptures to find daily readings, and songs would often flood my mind. As the month wore on, I would continue to have those internal battles, but the Lord was so kind to encourage my heart. Family and friends would comment to tell me they were up and waiting for the day's post. My mom and several friends even encouraged me to put the devotionals into a book. (Thank you for always believing in me, Mama!)

Over the course of that month, I witnessed firsthand how when the Lord gives us a task, He will provide all that is needed to complete it. As Christmas drew closer, I felt an awe and a wonder that I hadn't experienced since childhood. I enjoyed December like I never had before. I found that there were rewards that came from my intentionality. I sat before doing. I had fun with my kids. We made a list of things we wanted to do together (and we got to do almost all of them). We baked and read books, cooked and crafted. It was almost as if the Lord multiplied my time. December of 2019 was a gift. A gift from Him, to me: His child. I rose early and enjoyed every minute that I spent in His presence.

This little book that you hold in your hands is the compilation of the words He gave me each day of December 2019. It is a tangible form of a dream come true as well. For all of my life, I have loved writing. It has always been a desire and a dream of mine to publish a piece. The Lord has answered my prayers and the desires of my heart in the most unexpected of ways. Isn't that so like Him?

My hope is that these short devotionals and daily Bible readings will help to draw you near(er) to the One we celebrate. Truly, there is no Christmas without Christ.

May He surprise you, reveal Himself to you, and provide for you. May He give you a deeper love for Himself and may He shift your gaze to things eternal. May He use you in mighty ways, as you walk in obedience to Him and His holy Word. May He give you a boldness to share and a desire to minister to those around you.

Merry Christmas!

With love,

Kristi Menashe

Simply Come

[C O M E] Advent is described by Noah Webster (1828) as "a coming; intended as a season of devotion, with reference to the coming of Christ in the flesh..." To celebrate Christ and His birth, we must first come TO Him. For me, that means carving out time to spend with Him: in the reading of His Word, in prayer, in thanksgiving. It means setting aside other things- things that may be pressing, but that are not necessarily important. It means getting up before the sun or the kids. It means opening up His Love Letter to me, and searching the Scriptures. It means dialogue and communion with Christ. Webster's definition of the word come is "to advance nearer, in any manner, and from any distance." During this season, it's actually quite possible to move away from Him. We can be pulled away by the decorating, the commercialism, and our list of to-dos. This season, we have to consciously make the effort to draw near, and to invite Him to have first place in our hearts, days, and lives. We must make the move toward Him. He promises to draw near to us when we draw near to Him. He promises to never leave or forsake us. He promises to come back for us.

The very first step this advent season is to simply come.

TODAY'S READING:

Matthew 6:10

Matthew 11:28

Luke 9:23

John 7:37

James 4:8

Revelation 3:20

DECEMBER 2

Believe

[B E L I E V E] Why is it that children so easily believe and trust, but we adults find it so hard? Is it because, as we grow up and experience hurt, pain, and loss, we become calloused? Is it because we haven't seen a miracle with our own eyes? Maybe we don't want to be disappointed when our dreams don't actually come true. Whatever the reason, we need to repent of it and fully trust that our God can and will do what He says! The Bible has a lot to say about belief/believing. A few verses that often resonate with me are Mark 9:23-9:24. Jesus said to him, "If you can believe, all things are possible to him who believes." Immediately the father of the child cried out and said with tears, "Lord, I believe; help my unbelief!" So often, I let worry and doubt creep in and overtake my "belief"...but our belief has to be more than just surface deep. It has to have deep roots- planted in and upon His Word and His promises. A new word stood out to me today in the passage in Mark. It says, "if you CAN believe." Surely, He has given us all we need so that we can believe. He wouldn't ask us to do it if He hadn't first equipped us. Children view this season as a time of magic and wonder, yet we tend to view it as a season of busyness and chaos. I encourage you today- to sit at His feet. Call out to Him in prayer. What is that "thing" that you're having trouble believing Him for? Once our belief is in Him, we must believe upon Him. "But without faith it is impossible to please Him, for he who comes to God must believe that He exists, and that He is a rewarder of those who diligently seek Him." (Hebrews 11:6) Friend, the Lord has never broken a promise and He has proven

Himself faithful time and time again.

Believe He can. Believe He will.

TODAY'S READING:

---

2 Chronicles 20:20

Mark 1:15

Mark 9:23-24

Mark 16:14-18

Luke 8:11-15

John 3:18

John 20:27

Galatians 3:22

DECEMBER 3

Search

[S E A R C H] Last night, my son brought home an extra credit assignment for chemistry class. It was a word search. We just needed to find 118 chemical elements (You know, easy words, like roentgenium and molybdenum!). I love word searches, so he handed me the paper and I spent about an hour scouring the page. The letters tended to run together but I do have a technique, if the words don't pop out at me. I woke up this morning and had a different word for today's devotional planned, but I believe the Lord put on my heart to save that word and make today's: search. It's not always fun to search for something. Many times, searching means we can't find something, or that we have lost an item. Therefore, we are on the hunt. When we are searching, we have intent. We examine deeply and we will often look high and low. I have to remind myself that it is much better for me if I spend an hour searching for the Living God (exploring His living Word!) than it is for me to spend an hour online searching for new shoes or for the perfect Christmas photo card. The Lord is using the writing of this devotional in a personal way in my life. He's calling me to slow down, and to enjoy the season. I really have to push back against the hustle and bustle and the expectations December holds. I urge you to start your day by searching His Word. Journal. Pray. Enjoy that cup of coffee as you rebel against that to-do list the day holds. It'll be soul-refreshing and life-giving.

P.S. Spoiler alert: He promises to be found when we search for Him!

TODAY'S READING:

Job 11:7-9

Psalm 77:6

Psalm 139

Jeremiah 17:10

Jeremiah 29:11-14

Lamentations 3:40

Luke 15:8-10

DECEMBER 4

Proclaim

DECEMBER 4

[P R O C L A I M] "To announce; to declare with honor; to utter openly; to make public..." These are just a few of Webster's definitions for proclaim. It was still dark out. I awoke before my alarm went off, and clear as day- this word came to mind. It wasn't a word I had previously written down or thought about. What followed was: Go, tell it on the mountain, over the hill and everywhere. Go, tell it on the mountain, that Jesus Christ is born! I am convicted, because as I think about the things I am so willing to proclaim, His Name is not often first off my tongue. I'll tell a friend, "You have got to read this book!" or "Home Goods has the cutest pillows right now!" I am quick to sing the praises of earthly and temporal things. What if the first thing I told people about was how good God is? It could be a simple "Have a great day!," a smile, or a "Merry Christmas! Jesus loves you!" What if I called a friend who's hurting and reminded her of WHO holds her life in the palm of His hand? There are so many things I can utter, announce, and declare. Lord, let it be You that I cry out about! One of my favorite verses is Psalm 19:14: "Let the words of my mouth and the meditation of my heart be acceptable in Your sight, O Lord, my strength and my Redeemer." Oh, Lord...please help me speak words that proclaim Your Name. Please cause my tongue to be a vessel that speaks life and love. May others see my life as a witness: We proclaim by the way we live, whether we realize it or not. Lord, bring opportunities- to tell of You and Your wonders, to remind others of why we celebrate Christmas. My prayer is that I can slow down enough to not miss out on an assignment He has given me. Maybe it's as simple as reminding my children of how amazing Christ is. Maybe it's going out of my way to notice

25

a store clerk and giving a word of encouragement. Maybe it's blessing someone with something tangible. Whatever it is- may I seize the opportunities put before me, and may you, precious child of God, proclaim His name this season and always.

Let my life proclaim his holy and mighty and powerful and wonderful and majestic Name!

TODAY'S READING:

Deuteronomy 32:3

Psalm 40:9~10

Isaiah 52:7

Isaiah 60:6

Acts 17:22-31

Romans 9:17

1 John 1:1-4

Bless

DECEMBER 5

[B L E S S] Usually, when I think of a blessing, I think of something tangible given to someone. It can be a word spoken as well. A few years back, I read a book called The Family Blessing. The book references the Old Testament and how fathers would put their hands on their children and speak a blessing over them. We started implementing this in our home. We haven't done it every single night, but we have been pretty consistent. When we forget, our kids remind us and ask for it. They look forward to that hand on the top of their head and a prayer of blessing spoken over their life. "The Lord bless you and keep you; The Lord make His face to shine upon you, And be gracious to you; The Lord lift up His countenance upon you, And give you peace." (Numbers 6:24-26) This passage, or a portion of it, is always part of the blessing we speak over our children. This morning, my son came down and did his Bible reading. I mentioned the family blessings to him. He's reading straight through the Bible and he said, "Oh! I just read that passage this morning!" I love it when the Lord works like that. As fun as it is to bless others, my focus needs to shift, to first bless my Lord. It's easy to think of all that He has blessed me with, but when I turn it around and ponder ways I can bless Him, it's weird for me. I think Big God...has everything...doesn't "need" anything...all powerful...how can little ole me bless Him?! But then, He reveals Scripture to me and "shows" me ways. Psalm 34:1 says, "Bless the Lord, O my soul; And all that is within me, bless His holy Name." So how can I bless Him? I can praise His Name, speak love and life, and I can walk in obedience to His Word. My life should be a blessing- to Him and to others. During this Christmas season, so many are hurting. We don't have to think too hard before ideas come to mind.

How can you bless the Lord AND someone else today?

TODAY'S READING:

Psalm 34:1, 8

Psalm 63:4-5

Psalm 115:12-13

Jeremiah 17:7-8

James 3:8-12

DECEMBER 6

Rest

DECEMBER 6

[R E S T] I know what you're thinking...Rest? Really? In December? There's no time for that! Well, don't shoot the messenger. The Lord calls us to rest, and desires that we rest in Him. He tells us in Matthew 11:28: "Come to Me, all you who labor and are heavy laden, and I will give you rest." We often try to carry our burdens alone (or with the help of a friend), but He wants us to come and to rest in Him. He should be our number one GO-TO! Part of Psalm 61:2 says..."When my heart is overwhelmed; Lead me to the rock that is higher than I." In this crazy busy, fast-paced world we live in, it is easy to become overwhelmed. It's easy to worry, to become distracted, and to skip the resting because we've got too much to do. Oh, that I might learn from my kids, who bring me a book to read and climb up into my lap. They sink into me, without a worry or a care. Jesus, help me to open Your Book...to feel Your arms wrapped around me, and to find rest in You. Help me to consciously slow down. The list will still be there waiting for me. I can't expect to be "all the things to all the people" if I haven't first spent time with You, resting in Your love. I love how Webster describes rest: "to be quiet; to pause; to be undisturbed; to be at peace..."
Creator of the Earth, even You rested!

Jesus, be near. Draw us to You- not just this month...but always!

TODAY'S READING:

Genesis 2:2

Exodus 33:14

Psalm 37:6-7a

Matthew 11:28-30

Hebrews 4

DECEMBER 7

Magnify

[M A G N I F Y] "Oh, magnify the Lord with me, And let us exalt His name together." (Psalm 34:3) What do you think of when you hear the word magnify? I think of a magnifying glass, and how it makes things bigger when we hold it up and look through it. You know by now that I love me some Webster (1828). He describes "to magnify" as "to make great or greater; to make great in representation; to extol; to exalt in description or praise; to elevate." We have an opportunity this season to look beyond ourselves, and to find ways to magnify the Lord. In Luke 1:46, Mary says..."My soul magnifies the Lord, And my spirit has rejoiced in God my Savior." This is so profound to me because Mary was a very young woman when the angel told her she would conceive and bear a Son. I cannot imagine being Mary and experiencing all of that. Her faith is astounding to me. The Song of Mary in Luke 1 is all about making His name great. She extols the Lord and tells of His might and His mercy. Whether we are sitting alone with the Lord or speaking to others, we can magnify Him. Our souls can magnify Him and our tongues can as well. He has done great things!

He sent His Son, He offers us salvation, and He has blessed us beyond measure. Magnify Him today!

2 Samuel 7:26

Psalm 35:27-28

Psalm 69:30

Luke 1:46-55

Acts 19:17

DECEMBER 8

Trust

[T R U S T] My kids have been doing "trust falls" a lot lately. We will be walking along and they'll just shout out, "Trust fall!" Whoever is behind them has to catch them before they move their foot back to steady themselves, or they fail the test. I'm sure you are familiar with the game. My youngest son is a master at this, and my older two are always amazed at how low he'll go. Of course, they've always caught him, so he has every reason to trust. When I think about how the Lord has "caught" me every time, I am humbled, because I don't always fall back without worry and doubt. I often fail the trust test. Proverbs 3:5 says, "Trust in the Lord with ALL YOUR HEART." Not with some. Not with a piece. ALL. That's pretty black and white. The verse goes on to say "And lean not on your own understanding." When we lean on our own understanding, we can easily become discouraged or give up hope. When I look back over my life, I cannot think of a single time that the Lord wasn't faithful to me. Sure, He has allowed things that I didn't particularly love or enjoy, and there have been trials and situations I wish could be erased, BUT He has always been faithful. Trust Him enough to fall into His arms today. He will never let you fall. He will always keep His Word!

Remember those hurting around you and encourage someone today to give their whole heart to Jesus!

Psalm 28:7

Psalm 37:3

Psalm 56:4

Proverbs 3:5-6

Isaiah 12:2

Isaiah 50:10

Ephesians 1:11-14

DECEMBER 9

Gather

DECEMBER 9

[G A T H E R] "And let us watch out for one another to provoke love and good works, not neglecting to gather together, as some are in the habit of doing, but encouraging each other, and all the more as you see the day approaching." (Heb. 10:24-25, CSB) The word Christmas means "to gather around Christ." Gathering together is the very heart of this season of celebrating Christ's birth! Traditions are preserved and memories are made when we gather. When I think about Jesus' earthly ministry and what's recorded in the Bible, I think of all the times people crowded around and gathered together- to see Him, to hear Him, to be healed by Him. Gathering, to me, means to be with, to be together, to meet. Webster's 1828 describes it as: collecting, uniting, and assembling. All of these words have a positive connotation, in my opinion. This season can hold so much joy...but for so many, it holds heartbreak and sadness. Loss and grief are magnified. Financial troubles become more apparent. These things can cause people to isolate themselves. Is there someone you can reach out to today? Who's hurting and needs an invitation to gather with you? Maybe you are the one hurting and you just want to keep to yourself. Let this be an encouragement for you- you'll always be blessed when you've spent time in fellowship with other believers. I love that Emmanuel is one of Jesus' names, and that it means "God with us."

He wants to be with us. He wants us to be in community with others; to gather together in His name. Merry CHRISTmas!

TODAY'S READING:

Isaiah 7:14

Matthew 18:20

Matthew 25:31-36

1 Corinthians 14:26

Hebrews 10:24-25

DECEMBER 10

Dwell

[D W E L L] I love decorating and making my home a comfortable dwelling place. Having a husband who is a general contractor helps, as we have been able to remodel and redo things in our home of fifteen years. It is easy for me to become fixated on this temporary place. It's fun to shop for decor, fluff pillows, and rearrange furniture. Here's the thing I must constantly remind myself of, though: This. Is. All. Temporal. When I die, I won't be taking my home, or anything in it, with me. The Lord wants me to dwell with Him. While I am on this earth, dwelling means He wants to "inhabit for a time." It means that I should be "fixed in attention." He desires that I "hang upon [Him] with fondness" and that I would be "residing" in Him (Webster, 1828). My current home is not my forever home. It is not my permanent dwelling place. Heaven is! Oh, that I might put more effort, time, and love into my dwelling with Christ than I do my dwelling in this temporal home. "Lord, who may abide in Your tabernacle? Who may dwell in Your holy hill? He who walks uprightly, And works righteousness, And speaks the truth in his heart." (Psalm 15:1-2) This is my prayer, Lord. Work in me. Lord, You came down from heaven! You became flesh. You dwell among us! You came that we might dwell eternally with You. Help me to meditate on this all year long and not just during this Christmas season. You humbled Yourself, You died upon the cross, You rose again...all because You love me.

You desire for me to live and dwell with You forever! Friend, the same is true for you!

TODAY'S READING:

Psalm 4:8

Psalm 37:3-4

Psalm 84

Psalm 91:9-10

Isaiah 33:5-6

John 1:14

2 Corinthians 6:16

Ephesians 3:14-21

Colossians 3:16-17

DECEMBER 11

Give

DECEMBER 11

[G I V E] By now, we have at least thought of what we are giving others this Christmas. You've likely made your list, and possibly even purchased some (or all) of what's on it. It is so fun to give, isn't it? We love watching that special someone light up, as they open something they've wanted or asked for. "If a son asks for bread from any father among you, will he give him a stone? Or if he asks for a fish, will he give him a serpent instead of a fish? Or if he asks for an egg, will he offer him a scorpion? If you then, being evil, know how to give good gifts to your children, how much more will your Heavenly Father give the Holy Spirit to those who ask Him?" (Luke 11:11-13) This passage came to mind after the Lord put today's word on my heart. Our God loves to give to us- and He gives good gifts (James 1:17)! He is the Giver of all that we have. So, what do we give to a God who has given everything to us? There is only one thing He wants from us: our hearts. He doesn't want just a piece either. He wants the whole thing. Lyrics came to mind a bit ago...'Lord, I give you my heart...I give You my soul...I live for You alone... every breath that I take...every moment I'm awake...Lord, have Your way in me.' As much as I love this song, I cannot sing it without conviction. Every breath? Every moment? I wish it were so. It is my prayer that He would continue to work in me, and to have His way in me. I can give my heart to the One who gave His only Son for me.

I can give my thanks, my praise, and my love to the One who hung on the cross and bled and died for me! Will you give Him yours?

TODAY'S READING:

Deuteronomy 6:4-9

Proverbs 23:26

Luke 6:38

Luke 12:48

John 3:16

John 6:33

John 10:11

Romans 6:23

1 Corinthians 2:12

2 Corinthians 9:6-15

Receive

[R E C E I V E] When I hear the word receive, I think of happy things- like receiving a gift or an award. (We can receive bad news or correction too, but today's focus is about receiving from the Lord.) In the book of Acts, Jesus tells the apostles: "But you shall receive power when the Holy Spirit has come upon you; and you shall be witnesses to Me in Jerusalem, and in all Judaea and Samaria, and to the end of the earth." How encouraging is this for us, that as we witness, we will receive power?! In Psalms we read: "He shall receive blessing from the Lord, And righteousness from the God of his salvation..." (Psalm 24:5) We receive countless blessings from Him! In Colossians 2:6-7, we are reminded: "As you therefore have received Christ Jesus the Lord, so walk in Him, rooted and built up in Him and established in the faith, as you have been taught, abounding in it with thanksgiving." There is no greater gift we could ever receive than the gift of salvation. It's up to us to decide whether we will accept it or not. Those that reject God's gift will receive judgment and death. Those that receive Jesus as Lord and Savior will receive an eternal inheritance! Each December, we sing: "Joy to the world, the Lord is come; Let earth receive her King!" I notice the word "let" here, and the bottom line is this: He offers us so much, but are we willing to receive it? Will we let Him work in us, bless us, correct us, use us? Will we be open to receiving all that He has for us, even when it's scary, difficult, or uncomfortable? He is the God who makes broken into beautiful. The God who makes all things new. The God who gives so generously and graciously! My prayer today is that I will willingly receive from Him, and that you will too!

Receive Him as Lord and then open your hands and heart to all that He wants you to receive from Him.

Matthew 21:21-22

John 1:10-13

John 16:23-24

John 20:19-23

2 Corinthians 6:1-2

Hebrews 12:28-29

1 John 3:22

Prepare

[P R E P A R E] It can be a lot of work to prepare for guests: Clean the house. Set the table. Cook the food. Wrap the gifts. Why, then, do we go to all the trouble? We do it because we love our families and our friends and we want to invite them IN. I love Luke's account of two sisters who invited Jesus into their home. Mary sits while Martha preps and serves. I can definitely relate more to Martha. She's busy and "distracted with much serving." (Luke 10:40) She's irritated with her sister for just sitting (I can't blame her...I would be too!). The thing is though- while Martha was preparing food, Mary was preparing her heart. In this account, Jesus tells Martha that the one sitting at His feet is the one who's doing the right thing. Ouch. When we sing Joy To The World, we sing: "Let every heart prepare Him room..." How can we prepare Him room? We, too, should sit at His feet first. Before we do anything else or prepare for anyone else. We can't pour from an empty cup, so how can we expect to prepare for and serve others if we haven't prepared our hearts before the Lord? I love that the Bible speaks of the things that the Lord prepares for us too! In Psalm 23 we read: "You prepare a table for me in the presence of my enemies." In several commentaries I find- He is our Host. He prepares a feast for us and even though we are surrounded by enemies, He has the power to provide and protect. John 14:1-3 speaks of preparations He is making for our eternal home. "Let not your heart be troubled; you believe in God, believe also in Me. In My Father's house are many mansions; if it were not so, I would have told you. I go to prepare a place for you, I will come again to receive you to Myself; that where I am, there you may be also." We can't even begin to fathom what that place will be like!

I want to be "busy" about my Father's business...preparing for eternity by first sitting at His feet and preparing room in my heart. I'm sure the same is true of you...

TODAY'S READING:

Matthew 25:34

Luke 2:25-32

1 Corinthians 2:9

Ephesians 2:8-10

Serve

DECEMBER 14

[S E R V E] Yesterday, I took my two little ones into a few stores with me. I made a purchase at one of the stores and the store clerk was extremely friendly, sweet, and kind. It wasn't over the top, but rather genuine. We recently had an excellent server at a local restaurant too. It was so noticeable both times that when we walked out, my kids even commented on how nice they were. "Service with a smile!" we say and companies tout. Yet, it's very apparent when we are actually served with one; when we are served kindly and with care. Matthew 20:28 tells us..."just as the Son of Man did not come to be served, but to serve, and to give His life as a ransom for many." Over and over in the Bible, we are reminded that we are here to serve. First, we are to serve our Savior...and then His people. "If anyone serves Me, let him follow Me; and where I am, there my servant will be also. If anyone serves Me, him my Father will honor." (John 12:26) I can't honestly say that I always serve with a smile. Sometimes, I would rather BE served. If I am feeling frustrated with my children- I'll serve them, albeit begrudgingly. When that young store clerk served us so well yesterday, I was reminded that we stand out when are kind, helpful, and humble. We have the power and ability to "set the tone" in any given situation. I love Colossians 3:23-24..."And whatever you do, do it heartily, as to the Lord and not to men, knowing that from the Lord you will receive the reward of the inheritance; for you serve the Lord Christ." Our goal, as we serve others, should ultimately be to serve the Lord. To please Him. To humble ourselves before Him. We should never serve to be seen or noticed, but to honor and glorify the Lord. Oh, that I might have a servant's heart. Oh, that I might serve Him by serving His people with genuine care, kindness, and love. We may never know how far-reaching our service is, this side of heaven, but may we try to serve with glad hearts, with smiles, and with love.

Our service can make a great impact in a world that needs Jesus!

TODAY'S READING:

Isaiah 49:3

Matthew 6:1-24

Matthew 23:11-12

Matthew 25:21-23

Mark 10:43-45

Romans 12:1-2

Ephesians 6:5-8

1 Peter 4:7-11

DECEMBER 15

Peace

DECEMBER 15

[P E A C E] "A state of quiet or tranquility; freedom from disturbance or agitation; freedom from internal commotion; freedom from private quarrels; heavenly rest; harmony..." and the list goes on (Webster, 1828). This is one of those mornings when the word came and I wasn't expecting it. And yet, it's such a good word for all of us. One of my favorite verses is Isaiah 26:3: "You will keep him in perfect peace, Whose mind is stayed on You, Because he trusts in You." I believe that verse goes hand in hand with Philippians 4:6-7....."Be anxious for nothing, but in everything by prayer and supplication, with thanksgiving, let your requests be made known to God; and the peace of God, which surpasses all understanding, will guard your hearts and minds through Christ Jesus." Oh, how He wants us to have that peace that only He can bring/give! There are so many things we worry about and fuss over. Our minds can wander. Our hearts can lead us astray. We must stand upon the truths in His Word!! It is my desire that the Prince of Peace (Isaiah 9:6) would reign in my heart, my home, my life. Not only do I desire that supernatural peace, that brings freedom, rest, and harmony, but I long for Romans 12:18 to be true of my life: "If it is possible, as much as depends on you, live peaceably with all men." Disturbances, anxieties, and quarrels can become magnified during the holidays. We have to consciously bring it all to the Lord and surrender. Whatever it is that's causing a lack of peace in your life, take it to Him in prayer. Post verses up and around as reminders.

If there is someone you need to make peace with, take that first step today.

TODAY'S READING:

Psalm 85:8

Psalm 119:165

Psalm 122:7-8

John 14:27

John 16:33

Romans 5:1-2

2 Corinthians 13:11

Galatians 5:22-23

Colossians 3:15-17

Shine

DECEMBER 16

[S H I N E] As a young church-going kid, I would sing, "This little light of mine, I'm gonna let it shine. Hide it under a bushel? No! I'm gonna let it shine. Don't let satan blow it out. I'm gonna let it shine!" The grown-up version of this song can be found in Matthew 5:14-16: "You are the light of the world. A city that is set on a hill cannot be hidden. Nor do they light a lamp and put it under a basket, but on a lamp stand, and it gives light to all who are in the house. Let your light so shine before men, that they may see your good works and glorify your Father in heaven." We are called to shine- not for our own glorification, but for our Father's! This world is so dark- it needs our light! I've heard it said that some people may never read the Bible- but they're watching us. We may be the only "Bible" they'll ever read. During this season there are so many who want to help the hurting, who cheerfully give a little extra, and who will go out of their way to bless someone else. And yet, this season can also bring out the worst in people. I was an eyewitness to grand theft in a large store last week. I was angered and saddened by the depravity. It's mind-blowing to me how people can be so wicked, evil, and immoral. My God is not surprised, though. He came to save the lost. He came as the Light of the World! I love Lauren Daigle's song, Light of the World. She sings: "Glory to the Light of the World. Glory, the Light of the World is here." I pray my light shines brightly and reflects Him! We are constantly laughing because our puppy is obsessed with lights and reflections. He chases them nonstop. Anytime the sun is shining and our cell phones are out, Gus is nearby- waiting for and watching the reflection. He doesn't take his eyes off of the light. If I shine it on the ground, he chases it and steps on it. He runs back and forth, wagging his tail and drooling in delight. This may be a silly illustration, but I can learn this from Gus:

Chase hard after that Light! Shine Him brightly! Follow the reflection and reflect Him!

Numbers 6:24-26

Psalm 119:135

Daniel 12:3

Matthew 13:43

John 1:1-5

Philippians 2:14-16

1 John 2:1-8

Wait

DECEMBER 17

[W A I T] Waiting is hard. I, for one, am not very patient and don't enjoy waiting all that much. Ha! I've been thinking about Mary this morning. I wonder if her pregnancy felt like an eternity to her. The angel appeared to tell her she would conceive and carry the Son of God. And then her wait began. She must have been so expectant during those months. So excited, nervous, hopeful. Though I wasn't carrying God's Son in my womb, my pregnancies seemed long. I couldn't wait to hold those precious boys in my arms. Going through the adoption process for our daughter was a whole different kind of waiting! It was arduous, difficult, and long (much longer than a pregnancy)! I wondered if I would ever hold my daughter in my arms. And then...the day finally came! I love this quote I heard a while back: "Don't waste your wait." While we are here on this earth, we are most likely waiting for something: for good news, for a prayer to be answered, for healing, for that job, for a baby, for that apology, for our prodigal to return, for restoration. Whatever IT may be that we are waiting for, our hearts should be expectant. The wait can be so hard that we lose hope. We become weary and tired. We begin to think 'it'll never happen.' We have to make sure our eyes remain fixed on Christ! "He gives power to the weak, And to those who have no might He increases strength. Even the youths shall faint and be weary, And the young men shall utterly fall, But those who wait on the Lord shall renew their strength; They shall mount up with wings like eagles, They shall run and not be weary, They shall walk and not faint." (Isaiah 40:29-31) Like children wait to unwrap their gifts on Christmas morning, eager and giddy with excitement, so should we be...as we wait for the Lord to work, to answer, to provide, to return!

He is faithful. He is good. He has a plan and a purpose! He is coming back for us, so while we eagerly await Him, let's not waste the time we have been given.

Psalm 27:14

Isaiah 8:17

Micah 7:7

Luke 12:35-40

Romans 8:22-25

Galatians 5:5

Philippians 3:20

Hebrews 9:28

DECEMBER 18

Remember

DECEMBER 18

[R E M E M B E R] My family teases me about my crazy memory. I am able to remember odd things like what I was wearing the day I met my would be brother-in-law for the first time, back in 2002, phone numbers from thirty years ago, embarrassing moments, like falling UP the stairs in high school in my Birkenstocks, and specific things people have said that hurt my feelings (I'll spare the quotes here). Memories evoke emotions. We can remember something or someone from the past and feel all the feels. Remembering makes us laugh; it makes us cry. Memories can bring happiness, sadness, contentment, anger, joy, etc.. The type of remembering I'm speaking of today is this: Remembering the Lord's past faithfulness. Remember WHAT He has done. Remember ALL He has done. When we think back over our lives, isn't there evidence of His hand? Times when we thought we couldn't/wouldn't make it through? And yet- here we are. I used to have a real problem with fear and worry. The Lord has been faithful to work in me over the years, and I'm happy to say that though I still have a long way to go, I'm not who I used to be in that department. When fear creeps in now, I arrest those thoughts and think back to His past faithfulness. I remember other times I was afraid- and how He provided, protected, answered, and saved. Maybe this Christmas isn't shaping up to be the one you wanted. Maybe you can remember a better time, a better season, or even a better year. Whatever season of life you're in, you have the capability of remembering what He has done for you. Remember the cross- and the ultimate price He paid. "Remember His marvelous works which He has done, His wonders, and the judgments of His mouth...." (1 Chronicles 16:12) Remember that He left Heaven to come as a baby, to die for our sins, and to rise again to give us life eternal!

Let's not forget Him this Christmas. Let's not get wrapped up in temporal things, but rather in His love for us!

Psalm 9:1

Psalm 20:7

Psalm 105:7-11

Psalm 119:49-56

Ecclesiastes 12:1

Isaiah 63:11-13

Luke 24:6-9

1 Corinthians 11:24

DECEMBER 19

Know

DECEMBER 19

[K N O W] "These things I have written to you who believe in the name of the Son of God, that you may know that you have eternal life, and that you may continue to believe in the name of the Son of God." (1 John 5:13) It's pretty awesome to me that the Creator of the Universe has given us the Bible. We can know for sure, that if we believe upon Him, we will have eternal life. Once we place our trust in Him, it's not a guessing game. We don't have to try to be "good enough" to make our way into heaven. We never could be. Last night, we attended our family Christmas service at church. At the end of his message, Pastor Jack gave everyone the opportunity to accept Jesus Christ as Lord and Savior. He then called those accepting Christ down to the front, so he could pray with them. My youngest son looked at me and asked if I was going down. I told him I wasn't because I had already accepted Jesus. I asked him if he had just accepted the Lord (knowing he made the decision for Christ years ago) and his answer was that he had just done it for the fifth time. As cute as it initially sounded to me that he was making extra sure, it made me think: Once we accept Him, we know where we are headed. We can be secure, knowing we are sealed. Once we make the decision to give our lives to Christ, it should be our desire to get to know Him. He wants to have an intimate relationship with us. It is my prayer that as each day passes, I would get to know the God who gave me life, the Lover of my soul, the One who I'll spend eternity with! I know, without a doubt, where I am going when I die (...and so does my little guy). Do you? As we head into a new year, we have the chance to grow in our faith, and to know our God on a deeper level.

He knows everything about us, down to the very number of hairs on our heads. He knows us better than we know ourselves- and He still loves us. In return, He desires that we know and love Him.

Job 19:25

Jeremiah 29:11-13

Jeremiah 31:33-34

John 17:3

Philippians 3:7-10

1 John 3:16-20

1 John 4:4-8

1 John 5:18-20

DECEMBER 20

Hope

[H O P E] "This HOPE we have as an anchor of the soul, both sure and steadfast..." (Hebrews 6:19) This verse always comes to mind when I think of the word hope. I often wonder what people without the Lord hope in. All the things of this world are passing away and if we don't have a hope of eternity, what then? What can one long for? Desire? Expect? Wait for? I love how this verse uses an anchor as the description for what our hope in Christ is like. Webster (1828) says to anchor is: "to fix or fasten on; to fix in a stable condition." We drop anchor in the sea so that we will be kept in one spot- that one desired location. When we are anchored, we don't float away. We are not tossed about. The anchor holds us firmly so that, even when the current pulls, we are not moved. This is how our faith should be. Hopeful. Tethered. Sure and steadfast. When we have hope in Christ alone, we will not be uprooted when the currents and winds threaten to pull us away. So many things in this world challenge our hope. Webster defines hope as: to place confidence in; to trust in with confident expectation of good. There have been situations in the past that haven't turned out the way I had hoped. I'm sure the same is true for you. Life doesn't always go the way we had planned. My prayer is that we would fix our gaze upon the Master Planner; that we would anchor ourselves to the Living Hope, so that when circumstances try to yank us away...we will not be moved. What are you hoping for this Christmas? (...and I'm not talking about something under the tree!) Don't lose hope. Make sure that anchor is buried deep. Hope is a beautiful thing. It keeps us moving forward. It keeps us grounded. It encompasses expectation, surrender, and trust as we wait.

Our one true Hope came at Christmas. His name is Jesus. He offers the hope of Heaven- and that Hope is the best we could ever receive!

TODAY'S READING:

Psalm 31:24

Psalm 119:147

Romans 4:16-21

Romans 5:1-5

1 Thessalonians 4:13-18

Titus 1:2

Titus 2:13

Hebrews 10:19-25

1 Peter 3:15-17

DECEMBER 21

Worship

[W O R S H I P] It might sound goofy but the Lord uses my dogs to teach me lots of spiritual analogies. (Get yourself a Golden Retriever or two and you'll know what I'm talking about!) Goldens, by nature, are loyal, loving, devoted, and quite needy! They've been dubbed "Velcro" because they must be near or attached to their people at all times. If I sit down, there's immediately a big wet nose nudging me to pet him. When I open my Bible, a paw plops onto my lap. A furry head then rests on the open pages. My point is this: my dogs are just doing what they were created to do. What if we were more like them? Doing what we were created to do? We were put on this earth to glorify the Lord. We were made to worship Him. Oh, how worthy He is! I am not worthy of worship, but my dogs don't know that. They see me as their provider, their protector, the one who loves them and cares most for them. They know how much I love them, and in return, they love me back. They can't wait to sit at my feet. They long to show me their love. I actually wasn't going to use my dictionary today, but then I felt a prompting in my heart. "To honor with extravagant love and extreme submission; as a lover; to perform acts of adoration." (Webster, 1828) I'm not equating us to dogs, but rather, suggesting we can learn from them. Worship starts with bowing- first of the heart, then of the knee. "And when they had come into the house, they saw the young Child with Mary His mother, and fell down and worshiped Him." (Matthew 2:11a) May we humble ourselves, submit to Him, and honor Him with our love. May we revere Him and His Word and glorify His holy name. Our worship should be constant and continuous.

Our hearts should always be bowed before our Lord and Savior. Exalt Him. Praise Him. Thank Him. He is worthy!

TODAY'S READING:

Psalm 95:6-7

Psalm 100

Matthew 2:2

John 9:31

Colossians 3:16-17

Revelation 4:8-11

Revelation 14:6-7

Treasure

[T R E A S U R E] Last night, we kept our yearly Christmas tradition of meeting up with old friends at a local shopping mall. The kids were given tickets to ride the carousel, so we walked through the mall to get to it. We walked past high end stores. I think my kids experienced some major culture shock. Name brands they'd only heard of and then a Porsche store. The kids begged to go inside. The store clerk was extremely friendly and allowed them to not only sit in the $165,000 car, but push all of the buttons too. Needless to say, they were enthralled. Matthew 6:19-21 says..."Do not lay up for yourselves treasures on earth, where thieves break in and steal; but lay up for yourselves treasures in heaven, where neither moth nor rust destroys and where thieves do not break in and steal. For where your treasure is, there your heart will be also." Walking through that mall was a reminder for me that things tarnish, break, lose their appeal. They go out of style, and get dents and scratches. I like nice things and the Lord is constantly having to work on me in this area. I have to check my heart often. Where is my treasure? What am I teaching my kids to treasure? What am I laying up for myself in heaven? Am I more focused on the things of this world or the things of Christ? I want to be someone who treasures time, making memories and collecting priceless moments. We do not get "do overs." The day ends and it's never to come again. My friend and I talked last night about how quickly the kids are growing and how fast time has passed us by. I'm sure the Christmas season makes us even more sentimental, but as we recalled times from fifteen years ago, when our firstborn sons were babies, we felt a sense of sadness for years gone by. In my trusty dictionary, I read that treasure is "something very much valued." What do I value most? Do I treasure my relationship with Christ? The moments given to me on this earth? My "stuff?" Luke 2:19 says, "But Mary treasured up all these things and pondered them in her heart." (NIV) She held the King of the World and treasured Him!

Oh Lord, that I may treasure YOU, and the time given to me to live for Your glory! Shift my gaze from things under the tree- up to You!

Job 23:12

Psalm 119:162

Isaiah 33:6

Matthew 19:21

2 Corinthians 4:7

1Timothy 6:17-19

DECEMBER 23

Rejoice

DECEMBER 23

[R E J O I C E] "Now in the sixth month the angel Gabriel was sent by God to a city of Galilee named Nazareth, to a virgin betrothed to a man whose name was Joseph, of the house of David. The virgin's name was Mary. And having come in, the angel said to her, "Rejoice, highly favored one, the Lord is with you; blessed are you among women!" (Luke 1:26-28) Now, I don't know about you- but after hearing such astounding news, I'm not sure my first inclination would be to rejoice. Scripture does say Mary was troubled but the angel answered her questions and after talking with him, Mary said: "Behold the maidservant of the Lord! Let it be to me according to your word." (Luke 1:38) I have so much to learn from Mary! Earlier this year, I got a tattoo (along with my mother). Mine is a peony and the word 'rejoice' is the stem to the flower. Now I have a permanent and daily reminder to rejoice. As a child, one of my favorite church songs was Rejoice in the Lord Always. This word means so much to me now because I've been in a long season of lacking joy. I can feel Him working in me, restoring it and I am beyond grateful. I'm thankful for a patient God, who doesn't condemn me, because let's face it: our joy and our rejoicing should come from a place deep within. It should not be dependent upon our circumstances. We rejoice in the Lord, not because of what we have/have been given, but because of who He is!! Joy isn't synonymous with happiness. Rejoicing can happen at all times. One of my favorite worship song's lyrics include, "Your praise will ever be on my lips." My rejoicing and yours should be constant. Always. Forever. Despite any unpleasant issues we have going on, we can rejoice. (We all have something. There is no such thing as the "perfect life," and social media isn't an accurate gauge for us.) We can rejoice because we have a God who loves us. A God who has a plan and a purpose in everything. A God who is faithful. A God who was willing to send His Son to bear my sin. A God who defeated death and will do it again.

Webster says rejoicing is "enjoying." I love this. I want to enjoy the Lord more and more. Don't you? Lord, give me a heart to enjoy You all my days!

TODAY'S READING:

Psalm 5:11

Psalm 33:1

Psalm 63:7

Isaiah 61:10-11

Zephaniah 3:17

John 16:19-23

Philippians 4:4

1 Thessalonians 5:16

1 Peter 1:6-9

DECEMBER 24

Love

DECEMBER 24

[L O V E] "If you love Me, keep My commandments." (John 14:15) If you love Me, feed My sheep." (John 21:17) "Greater love has no one than this, than to lay down one's life for his friends." (John 15:13) "These things I command you, that you love one another." (John 15:17) The Bible makes it pretty clear for us: "By this all will know that you are My disciples, if you have love for one another." (John 13:35) To me, this verse means that others will be able to see "fruit" by looking at us and by watching us. The way I love, or don't love, is on display- whether I like it or not. I have the opportunity to show and to bestow love to everyone around me. So do you. I am constantly telling my kids these things too....especially "if you love Me, you'll obey me." One thing that keeps coming to mind, though, is this: my love for the Lord comes first. I simply cannot love others without loving Him first and foremost. My love for Him should not be forced. I shouldn't sit and read the Word because I feel like I "have" to. My love for Christ shouldn't feel dutiful, like I'm checking boxes off my list. I've struggled with this my whole life. With feeling like He couldn't possibly love me as much when I am not as consistent in reading, in prayer, or in my devotion to Him. However, this is not true! His love is not waning. It does not change, fade, or waver. I am human and my love does fail. It disappoints. Thank God He's always working in me, giving me chances to grow. He's doing the same in your life! Each day, the goal is to love better, to love deeper, to love more. When I love Jesus, my love for everyone else will grow too. My "fruit" will become more and more evident and those around me will feel it. I often have to ask Him to give me more love- for Him, for His Word, for His people. The greatest gift we can give? His love. The greatest gift we can receive? His love.

Oh Jesus, thank you for coming down to earth as a baby-Pure Love in the flesh. Thank You for exhibiting perfect love on the cross. Thank You for rising again, showing us that Your love is alive. Thank You for another day- to love You and to love others.

TODAY'S READING:

Deuteronomy 6:4-9

Proverbs 17:17

Jeremiah 31:3

John 3:16

1 Corinthians 13:1-13

1 Corinthians 16:14

Ephesians 4:1-3

1 Peter 4:8

1 John 4:7-21

DECEMBER 25

Adore

[A D O R E] Merry Christmas!! Our advent began with an encouragement to "simply come" and it ends with a call to adore Him. O come let us ADORE Him! The King of Kings, Lord of Lords, our Great Shepherd, the Morning Star. He is so worthy of our adoration...not just today, but everyday!! On this Christmas morning, I'll leave you with the lyrics of my favorite Christmas song. I love it so much that I listen to it year round:

So much wonder lay before us...In a manger, Heaven's here... Earth is longing for its Savior...Highest King, humble frame, now appeared...Unto us a Child is born...Unto us the Savior of the world...We adore You, we adore You...Unto us a Child is born...Unto us the Savior of the world...We adore You, we adore You, Lord...Stars of glory break the shadows...Leading all to Perfect Light...Shepherds gathered bearing witness...To the hope of the world, Jesus Christ...Unto us a Child is born...Unto us the Savior of the world...We adore You, we adore You...Unto us a Child is born...Unto us the Savior of the world...We adore You, we adore You...We adore You...Now behold Him, precious Jesus... Our Redeemer, Mary's Son...God incarnate, You are with us... Prince of Peace, Emmanuel, Promised One...Unto us a Child is born...Unto us the Savior of the world...We adore You, we adore You...Unto us a Child is born...Unto us the Savior of the world... We adore You, we adore You...All I want to do is adore You... We adore You...Majesty, Holy One...Prince of Peace...We adore You!!

TODAY'S READING:

_____

Enjoy reading Luke 2:1-20 as a family!

Have a blessed day celebrating Jesus Christ!

Kristi and her husband, Josh, live in Southern California with their four children. Kristi homeschools, and is a co-leader for the Established ministry at Calvary Chapel Chino Hills. Kristi enjoys traveling, mentoring other women, and hosting Bible studies in her home. She is an avid reader, and has had a lifelong passion for writing.

Made in the USA
Monee, IL
04 November 2020

46673789R00083